Sister Jan,

May You Be
Nourished +

Blessed.

Marlene R. Scott

Keeping It Real

The Straight and Narrow

MARLOWE R. SCOTT

Keeping It Real
The Straight and Narrow

Marlowe R. Scott

Pearly Gates Publishing LLC, Houston, Texas

Keeping It Real
The Straight and Narrow

ISBN 10: 1945117125
ISBN 13: 978-1945117121
Library of Congress Control Number: 2016942445

For information and bulk ordering, contact:
Pearly Gates Publishing LLC
Angela R. Edwards, CEO
P.O. Box 62287
Houston, TX 77205
BestSeller@PearlyGatesPublishing.com

Dedication

This book is dedicated to all Christians making the journey to the Cross leading to our Heavenly Home and to those yet to be saved who will join in the journey.

Acknowledgments

Always giving praises and thanks to our Lord and Savior Jesus Christ for all He continues to do in my life and the lives of others touched through the gifts given to me.

To my daughter, Angela R. Edwards, the CEO of Pearly Gates Publishing, LLC: Much love for your continued ministry through using your many talents to uplift God's Kingdom.

For those who have taken the time to provide endorsements and words of encouragement, I sincerely **THANK EACH OF YOU**. May this book also provide spiritual nourishment to you and those you touch.

A Special Note from President Obama & Family

In September 2015, President Barak Obama and family were given an autographed copy of *Spiritual Growth: From Milk to Strong Meat,* the first book that became an Amazon Best Seller. The Obamas sent a note of appreciation stating in part:

"Thank you for your gift. It was such a nice gesture, and we were touched by your generosity. Your thoughtfulness reflects the extraordinary kindness of the American people. More than anything, please know that your kind words and support for our shared values motivate us each and every day."

Preface

The writing of *Keeping It Real: The Straight and Narrow* could not be written without remembering a special evangelist I worshipped with for many years. She possessed many genuine Christian qualities within my view, with the primary being godly wisdom. She ardently studied scriptures, mentored many, possessed a spirit of humbleness, taught God's Word clearly, and preached deep truths without wavering.

That special human vessel regularly spoke about "unction"- a word you may not hear too often today. Unction is the act of anointing as a sign of consecration; also a soothing ointment; a manner indicating or arousing emotion, especially religious fervor. She always had oil with her for anointing, would willingly pray for anyone anywhere at any time, and was highly respected by ministers who listened to and used her wise counsel.

Keeping It Real: The Straight and Narrow

She was a regular teacher at Black Rock Retreat Center, Quarryville, Pennsylvania in Lancaster County where we experienced many mountaintop experiences together. Although she has gone on to her Heavenly reward, she has left a legacy that will live on in those lives she touched. She constantly emphasized being "real" and that people must stop "playing church".

Introduction

The inspiration and title for this book were given to me in September 2015. *Keeping It Real: The Straight and Narrow* has been a spiritual work in progress (so to speak) as is our journey to our Heavenly Home. The cross depicted on the front cover aptly represents the Cross bore on Calvary by our Lord and Savior, Jesus Christ.

There is a well-loved and widely sung hymn of the church, *The Old Rugged Cross* by George Bennard, the words of which resonate deep in my soul as I sing or hum them. All verses and chorus are shared here, as they have deep meanings and truths for "Real" believers in Jesus Christ.

Keeping It Real: The Straight and Narrow

Old Rugged Cross
By: George Bennard

Keeping It Real: The Straight and Narrow

Old Rugged Cross

On a hill far away stood an old rugged cross,
The emblem of suffering and shame;
And I love that old cross where the dearest and best
For a world of lost sinners was slain.

CHORUS:
So I'll cherish the old rugged cross,
Till my trophies at last I lay down;
I will cling to the old rugged cross,
And exchange it some day for a crown.

O that old rugged cross, so despised by the world,
Has a wondrous attraction for me;
For the dear Lamb of God left his glory above
To bear it to dark Calvary.

In that old rugged cross, stained with blood so divine,
A wondrous beauty I see,
For 'twas on that old rugged cross Jesus suffered and died,
To pardon and sanctify me.

To that old rugged cross I will ever be true,
Its shame and reproach gladly bear;
Then he'll call me some day to my home far away,
Where his glory forever I'll share.

Note: When I was married in 2006, Rev. Richard W. Jones suggested using our beautiful main sanctuary at Tabernacle Baptist Church in Burlington, New Jersey. I told him I wanted to get married in the chapel, which was a part of the older church. It was intimate and has a rugged cross suspended in the front. This represented what my heart desired and we were married there. Sometime before getting married, an evangelist I had known for some time told me the story of how the cross came to be. It was created by Richard A. Timbers, Sr. He would collect driftwood from the nearby Delaware River in Burlington, New Jersey and create beautiful works of art.

In preparing to write this book, I was inspired at my kitchen table to include the uplifting hymn *How to Reach the Masses* (also known as *Lift Him Up)*. In checking a familiar website I use to gather background information, I discovered an amazing fact! The composer of this popular hymn was Johnson Oatman, Jr. who was born April 21, 1856 near Medford, New Jersey - which is only 20 minutes from my home! I was so excited, I called friends and relatives with my new knowledge.

Mr. Oatman was a member of a Methodist church, became an Ordained Minister, and is credited with **thousands** of compositions! Other well-known hymns credited to him are: *Count Your Blessings, Higher Ground* (also known as *I'm Pressing On the Upward Way), No, Not One,* and *The Last Mile of the Way.* For our local Burlington County New Jersey residents, we know individuals who attended the New Jersey Collegiate Institute in Bordentown - as did Mr. Oatman. He married Wilhelminia Reid and had three children: Rachel, Miriam, and Percy. Johnson Oatman, Jr. died September 25, 1922 at the age of 66.

Two of Mr. Oatman's hymns are included in this book. For those who know the melodies, why not pause and sing or hum to yourself as you meditate on and soak in the words? That is what I do frequently. I find peace and comfort in both the words **and** melody.

Lift Him Up
By: Johnson Oatman, Jr.

Lift Him Up

How to reach the masses, men of every birth,
For an answer, Jesus gave the key:
"And I, if I be lifted up from the earth,
Will draw all men unto Me."

Refrain:
Lift Him up, lift Him up;
Still He speaks from eternity;
"And I, if I be lifted up from the earth,
Will draw all men unto Me."

Oh! The world is hungry for the Living Bread,
Lift the Savior up for them to see;
Trust Him, and do not doubt the words that He said,
"I'll draw all men unto me."

Don't exalt the preacher, don't exalt the pew,
Preach the Gospel simple, full, and free;
Prove Him and you will find that promise is true,
"I'll draw all men unto Me."

Lift Him up by living as a Christian ought,
Let the world in you the Savior see;
Then men will gladly follow Him Who once taught,
"I'll draw all men unto Me."

Keeping It Real: The Straight and Narrow

As you read, contemplate, and digest the message of this book, may it inspire you and improve your relationship with Jesus as here on Earth, we strive - step by step up our personal mountains - to reach our Heavenly Home.

You are encouraged to make notes and respond to the questions at the end of each chapter. They are there to remind you of times when you may have been blessed and inspired, as well as to share your thoughts with others.

This book moves along the journey one must travel on the *'Straight and Narrow'* through the sharing of scriptures, stories, illustrations, and poems. May you come to know (as I have) the dry and rough places on the journey ultimately end. The lessons learned become testimonies and evidence of Jesus' unending love for us until we meet Him face to face.

KEY SCRIPTURES

"The voice of him that crieth in the wilderness, prepare ye the way of the Lord, make straight in the desert a highway for our God.
Every valley shall be exalted, and every mountain and hill shall be made low: and the crooked shall be made straight, and the rough places plain:
And the glory of the Lord shall be revealed, and all flesh shall see it together: for the mouth of the Lord hath spoken it."

Isaiah 40:3-5 KJV

"Enter ye in at the strait gate: for wide is the gate, and broad is the way, that leadeth to destruction, and many there be which go in thereat:
Because strait is the gate, and narrow is the way, which leadeth unto life, and few there be that find it."

Matthew 7:13-14 KJV

Keeping It Real: The Straight and Narrow

Table of Contents

CHAPTER ONE
KEEPING IT REAL

What does "real" mean? It is something true, actual, genuine, authentic, and sincere. "Narrow" is defined as a path or way with a little 'wiggle room' to go left, right, or to even do a complete turn around. In the context of this writing, the "Real Narrow" way leads to life – **eternal life**.

I admit: There are paths in life which may be wider and easier to humanly travel, but those paths do **not** lead to the Cross of Calvary and eternal life. The wider paths may include such things associated with wayward friendships, hang-ups, greed, habits, and those sins and wrongs set out clearly in the Holy Scriptures.

There are many imitations in today's world that **look** like and **appear** to be the real thing:
  ➢ Furs
  ➢ Leather coats and handbags
  ➢ Jewelry
  ➢ Imitation foods – i.e. butter and sugar
  ➢ Artificial turf on sports fields
  ➢ Imitation flavorings
  ➢ Building materials – i.e. marble, brick, and wood - that *appear* real.

Likewise, sometimes during church worship, some unreal things may occur. Scripture addresses them clearly in the speaking of vain words, religious traditions and rituals instituted by man, judging others by their outward appearance or circumstance, and singing songs without believing or applying those words to our lives.

There may also be other reasons, such as those who imitate what others do and feel that is the way to worship. There could be newly-converted Christians in the midst who do not yet understand how to interpret and apply scripture to resist the numerous temptations of the world and deceptions of the devil.

I heard some time ago that the higher our spiritual level becomes, the harder the devil tries to tempt and hinder our journey. For those who read my previous book, *Believing Without Seeing: The Power of Faith*, you are familiar with and have read the addendum at the end about Satan, the fallen angel cast out of Heaven by God.

Keeping It Real

Questions for Consideration

1. When you have perceived "unreal" things in church, how have you ignored them and remained focused on the worship service?

_____

_____

_____

_____

_____

_____

_____

_____

_____

_____

_____

_____

_____

_____

2. How have religious traditions hindered your growth and understanding of true worship?

_____

_____

_____

_____

_____

_____

_____

_____

_____

_____

_____

_____

_____

_____

_____

_____

CHAPTER TWO
THE DEVIL GOES TO CHURCH

The Devil Goes to Church

As shared in prior writings, my mother had many talents and was often invited to sing or recite poetry in church as well as civic programs. The reading of the following poem was requested **many** times. It is from a collection of poetry entitled *Alabaster Boxes* by Bessie Brent Winston (copyrighted in 1947).

The poem's title is *The Devil Goes to Church*. It shows qualities and temptations presented to ourselves and others as we travel our personal path to the cross. The poem is written in a form known as 'satire', which effectively uses humor to show weaknesses, bad qualities, and sarcasm to make its point.

THE DEVIL GOES TO CHURCH

The devil went to church one day,
And as he strolled along
He planned how he could execute
Some deeds of sin and wrong.
He did not stop down near the door,
As most outsiders would,
But went as close as he could get
To where the preacher stood.

He heard him read in earnest tones
Words from the Holy Book;
The devil turned and hurled at him
An ugly, angry look.
He heard him tell with gentle voice
The curse of sin and pain,
And strive to bring the straying sheep
Back to the fold again.

He heard him tell in wisdom's words
Salvation's wondrous plan.
The devil frowned and bit his lip
And said, "I hate that man.
I've done my best by day and night
To lead this flock astray;
He'll undo everything I've done,
If he goes on this way."

The Devil Goes to Church

So down the aisle he made his way
To see what he could do
Along the line of starting things
And making trouble brew.
He saw two girls down near the door,
With faces sweet and fair,
With heads bowed low, as if they were
In earnest, thoughtful prayer.

Straight to those girls the devil went
And said, "Look at that hat
That Sister Molly Gray has on,
And Easter day at that!"
Then up from thoughts of prayer and praise
Two pair of roguish eyes
Went straight to Sister Molly's hat
In mischievous surprise.

And then they bowed their heads again
And laughed and giggled till
The deacon had to go to them
And ask them to be still.
And then the devil took a seat
By Sister Mary Wood;
He knew she'd much prefer to hear
The bad instead of good.

Keeping It Real: The Straight and Narrow

He whispered something in her ear,
And then she turned her head
And whispered to the deacon's wife,
I don't know what she said,
But instantly the deacon's wife
Replied, "O dear, O dear,
If that is true, then I'll not pay
Another penny here."

The devil grinned and went his way,
His joy too deep to tell,
And as he went he murmured low,
"That worked out pretty well."
And then he went to Brother Green -
He'd seen him yawn and gap.
He said, "Just lean your head on me,
And take a little nap."

He gently rocked him to and fro
Down dreamland's pathway steep
And sang him impish lullabies
Till he was fast asleep.
He saw a small boy passing by,
On some dire mischief bent;
Then down the aisle and through the door
A wireless was sent.

The Devil Goes to Church

It read like this: "Peep in the door
At good old Silas Blair;
He'll kneel in just a little while
To make a silly prayer.
Just keep an eye, and when he does,
You throw a stone and run.
It won't be wrong, for every boy
Must have a little fun."

And so it happened that a stone
Came whizzing through the air
And made poor Brother Silas jump
And yell out in despair.
An Amen brother, stanch and true,
Whose name was Aaron Kent,
Had in his worn-out pocketbook
A dollar and a cent.

He hadn't been to church for months,
And so had planned to spare
The dollar bill to sort of pay
For times he wasn't there.
The devil sat down by his side
And whispered in his ear,
"You're just as crazy as a bat
To pay that dollar here.

Keeping It Real: The Straight and Narrow

"The church clerk and the treasurer, too,
Are crooked as can be,
They always take their spending change
From out of the treasury.
Where do you think the treasurer's wife
Gets all her fancy clothes?
She never does a lick of work,
But dresses up and goes.

"That clerk has got a brand new car,
All shiny, black and sleek;
Folks don't go in for cars like that
On twenty-five per week.
So take your dollar bill straight home
And put your penny in;
To help those crooked folks along
Would really be a sin."

So when the plate was passed around,
Good Brother Aaron Kent
Kept back the nice new dollar bill
And gave the church the cent.
The devil smacked him on the back
And said, "That's fine, old dear,
And don't you ever, ever give
More than a penny here."

The Devil Goes to Church

A little girl named Rosabelle,
Who came from Tennessee,
Was chairman of a junior club
They called The Busy Bee.
The club had labored faithfully
Through each hot summer day,
Till twenty-four bright bills
In their small treasury lay.

The devil said to Rosabelle,
"That hat at Kimberly's
Has been reduced to four-nineteen;
It's pretty as can be.
Why don't you go and get that hat
Before Jane Spencer does?
She always thinks she looks so nice;
Don't hesitate, because

"Part of that money's yours by rights;
You worked just like a mule;
To give the church the whole of it,
You'd be a little fool."
And so on next church meeting day,
The lovely Rosabelle
Was dressed up in a brand new hat,
And purse and gloves as well.

Keeping It Real: The Straight and Narrow

He found his way up in the choir,
Where only peace belongs,
And sitting down cross-legged, went
To meddling with the song
He whispered in a sister's ear,
"This isn't fair a bit;
Unless they sang the hymns I liked,
If I were you, I'd quit.

And then an ugly selfish look
Came in that sister's eyes,
And made the organist look up
In sad and grave surprise.
He made the tenors laugh and talk
Till there was not a trace
Of order in the choir stand;
It bordered on disgrace.

He then walked up and down the aisle
And looked at everyone,
To see if there was anything
That he had left undone.
He really wasn't satisfied;
He could have spent the day,
Rejoicing in his devilment
And leading folks astray.

The Devil Goes to Church

The sermon being over now,
The devil got his hat
And said, "I wish I'd had more time,
But 'twasn't bad at that."
And when he snuggled down to sleep,
His imps all heard him say,
"I'm tired as a man can be,
But what a happy day!"

~ The End ~

Keeping It Real: The Straight and Narrow

Questions for consideration

1. I have personally done some of those things cited in this poem, from youth to adulthood. How has this poem made you more aware of doing the same things in church?

_____

_____

_____

_____

_____

_____

_____

_____

_____

_____

_____

_____

_____

_____

_____

The Devil Goes to Church

2. What do you feel is the overall message of this poem?

_____

_____

_____

_____

_____

_____

_____

_____

_____

_____

_____

_____

_____

_____

_____

CHAPTER THREE
MOUNTAIN CLIMBING

Mountain Climbing

In preparing to climb mountains on Earth, you need the correct footwear, ropes, walking sticks, backpack, food, and water - to name a *few* essentials. During the ascent, you may encounter slippery rocks, streams, waterfalls, caves, briers, snakes, stinging insects, and wild animals. Along the way, there may also be welcomed plateaus for rest or insurmountable obstacles.

For the climb we must take on our **spiritual** journey, we also need supplies and weapons to combat snares, hardships, hurts, and pains we face. Spiritual armor for this type of mountain climbing and battle is found in Ephesians 6:10-18. A fuller discussion on that passage of scripture was presented in my first publication, *Spiritual Growth: From Milk to Strong Meat,* and also shares valuable information learned from a class on Spiritual Warfare. God has provided spiritual armor for us. To stay battle-ready, we must study scriptures, pray, hear Christ-centered preaching, worship God, and fellowship regularly with believers while learning how to apply and use what God has given us for combat!

Keeping It Real: The Straight and Narrow

For *seasoned* Christians, you may identify with the journey to the Cross of Calvary. For *newer* Christians, they will learn that trials, temptations, and worldly turmoil will happen, but be assured: Jesus will be with you every step you take and with each burden you bear.

In the New Testament, Jesus illustrated many truths through His telling of parables. A brief definition of a parable is that it is a short story teaching a spiritual or moral lesson or truth. For the following story, there is a literary term called an 'allegory' which represents a quality or idea in the likeness of a person or thing, to be interpreted *symbolically*.

Such is the story I read years ago: *The Pilgrim's Progress*. It tells the experience of the main character, Christian, striving to reach the Celestial City - his Heavenly destination. Following is a brief summary.

Mountain Climbing

THE PILGRIM'S PROGRESS
John Bunyan (written 1678)

The story has several terms Christians may be able to identify with. The main character is Christian. He started the journey to the Celestial City (also called Mount Zion). He had to make the journey alone because his family would not accompany him. He went through such places and the "Slough of Despondent", "Valley to Humiliation", "Valley of the Shadow of Death", and mountains of "Error and Caution". He, at one point, is sheltered in 'Goodwill's' home where he learns about faith. He also meets three 'Shining Ones' and four mistresses of the 'Palace Beautiful' who shelter him and give him weapons.

Along the way, he encounters Apollyon and uses a sword to ward him off. The story continues through others' personal encounters, to include 'Shepherds' who inform him that others have died trying to reach the Celestial City and warned him to be aware of shortcuts which may actually be paths to Hell. Christian finally reaches the Land of Beulah along with a companion he picked up earlier, but they must cross a river. With some struggles, they make it safely across and are welcomed into the Celestial City by its residents.

There is more to the story, but reading the **actual** book is more fulfilling. Points that may be drawn from this brief summary are:

1. We may not be able to take loved-ones on our spiritual journey.
2. God will supply help from unexpected sources along the way.
3. You are given weapons to combat the devil.
4. Temptations will try to hinder your progress.
5. The closer you get to the goal, the stronger opposition will be.
6. There is a river to cross referred to as the "River of Life" in the Book of Revelation.
7. When you reach Heaven, you WILL BE WELCOMED!

Mountain Climbing

Questions for Consideration

1. What mountains and hindrances have you experienced in your journey?

_____

_____

_____

_____

_____

_____

_____

_____

_____

_____

_____

_____

_____

_____

_____

2. How did you overcome them?

_____

_____

_____

_____

_____

_____

_____

_____

_____

_____

_____

_____

_____

_____

_____

_____

Mountain Climbing

3. Did you question the "why" of your problems when you felt you didn't deserve them?

_____

_____

_____

_____

_____

_____

_____

_____

_____

_____

_____

_____

_____

_____

_____

_____

4. As you have grown in your spiritual walk, does looking back let you know you are stronger?

_____

_____

_____

_____

_____

_____

_____

_____

_____

_____

_____

_____

_____

_____

_____

_____

CHAPTER FOUR
HIGH PLACES

High Places

When thinking about the song *Lift Him Up* that was shared earlier, my thoughts went to those scriptures about hind's feet in high places, because the Cross of Jesus was erected on Calvary – a high place for ALL to see.

The following scriptures speak of having our feet set on high places - mountains for example - like a hind. Again, my desire to learn more lead to researching what a "hind" is and I discovered an astonishing fact: The hind is a female deer of the red deer species. The male of the species is called a hart. As with many of God's creation, the hind's size varies due to the geographical location in which she lives. She generally weighs between 120 to 170 pounds.

2 Samuel 22:32-37 (KJV)

32. For who is God, save the LORD?

and who is a rock, save our God?

33. God is my strength and power:

and he maketh my way perfect.

34. He maketh my feet like hinds' feet:

and setteth me upon my high places.

35. He teacheth my hands to war; so that a

bow of steel is broken by mine arms.

36. Thou hast also given me the shield of thy salvation:

and thy gentleness hath made me great.

37. Thou hast enlarged my steps under me;

so that my feet did not slip.

High Places

Psalms 18:31-35 (KJV)

31. For who is God save the LORD?

Or who is a rock save our God?

32. It is God that girdeth me with strength,

and maketh my way perfect.

33. He maketh my feet like hinds feet,

and setteth me upon my high places.

34. He teacheth my hands to war, so that a

bow of steel is broken by mine arms.

35. Thou hast also given me the shield of thy salvation:

and thy right hand holden me up,

and thy gentleness hath made me great.

High Places

Habakkak 3:17-19 (KJV)

17. Although the fig tree shall not blossom, neither shall fruit be in the vines; the labour of the olive shall fail, and the fields shall yield no meat; the flock shall be cut off from the fold, and there shall be no herd in the stalls:
18. Yet I will rejoice in the LORD,
I will joy in the God of my salvation.
19. The LORD God is my strength, and he will make my feet like hinds' feet, and he will make me walk upon mine high places. To the chief singer on my stringed instruments.

These scriptures give important spiritual lessons on being like a hind:

➢ Our feet will not slip – go backward down the mountains we have climbed.

➢ With strength and perfection, we are blessed to set in high places and taught to fight spiritual battles with proper armor and support.

➢ We are to rejoice in the Lord - no matter what is going on around us - and continue walking in those high places.

Keeping It Real: The Straight and Narrow

Questions for Consideration

1. In addition to the three scriptural passages stated, how does the hind relate to your Christian journey?

_____

_____

_____

_____

_____

_____

_____

_____

_____

_____

_____

_____

_____

_____

_____

2. Scripture often uses God's creation to teach valuable lessons. Take a few minutes to jot down other animals or vegetation used to teach us.

_____

_____

_____

_____

_____

_____

_____

_____

_____

_____

_____

_____

_____

_____

_____

_____

3. Both the Old (2 Samuel 22:36 and Psalm 18:35) and New Testaments (Ephesians 6:13-17) speak of spiritual armor. When have you used spiritual armor to overcome the wiles of the devil?

_____

_____

_____

_____

_____

_____

_____

_____

_____

_____

_____

_____

_____

_____

CHAPTER FIVE
PRESSING UPWARD

Pressing Upward

Much like the Epistle of Paul in Philippians 3:14, Christians are to "press" to the mark of the prize of the high calling of God in Jesus Christ. Another great hymn by Johnson Oatman, Jr. is fitting to note: *Higher Ground* (also known as *I'm Pressing on the Upward Way*).

HIGHER GROUND

I'm pressing on the upward way,
New heights I'm gaining every day;
Still praying as I'm onward bound,
"Lord, plant my feet on higher ground."

Refrain:
Lord, lift me up and let me stand,
By faith, on Heaven's tableland,:
A higher plane that I have found;
Lord, plant my feet on higher ground.

My heart has no desire to stay
Where doubts arise and fears dismay;
Though some may dwell where those abound,
My prayer, my aim, is higher ground.

I want to live above the world,
Though Satan's darts at me are hurled;
For faith has caught the joyful sound,
The song of saints on higher ground.

I want to scale the upmost height
And catch a gleam of glory bright;
But still I'll pray till heav'n I've found,
"Lord, plant my feet on higher ground."

Pressing Upward

CALVARY'S CROSS – A POEM

Jesus Christ gives us eternal life through His bearing of our sins on the Cross of Calvary in a place also called Golgotha (The Place of the Skull). The following poem, *Calvary's Cross*, shares my attempt to convey a message to point others to Our Savior Jesus Christ.

CALVARY'S CROSS
Marlowe R. Scott © 2016

The song writer wrote there's a cross for everyone
Yes, crosses for you and me
The crosses we bear may be many
But each has a message and lesson you see.

There is a cross that is more precious than them all
It is The Cross on Calvary
That rugged Cross that Our Savior bore
To save sinners like you and me.

Jesus was crucified on that cross
On the hill named Calvary.
As between two sinners the cross stood
As He bore the sins for you and me.

He died and was placed in a borrowed tomb
Where His body stayed until early on the third day
Then, He rose with all authority in Heaven and earth
On that very first Easter Day!

After 40 days before His ascension to Glory
Jesus promised the Holy Spirit's power would come
So that mankind would become witnesses in all the Earth
Because of Salvation given by God's One and Only Son.

Now, we must seek forgiveness and tell the world
That the free gift of Salvation is here
To anyone admitting sin and believing in Jesus
The One who sacrificed His life because He loved us so dear.

Pressing Upward

Questions for Consideration

1. How have songs and/or poetry blessed and comforted you spiritually?

_____

_____

_____

_____

_____

_____

_____

_____

_____

_____

_____

_____

_____

_____

_____

2. What are some of your favorites? Why not take time to share them with family and friends?

_____

_____

_____

_____

_____

_____

_____

_____

_____

_____

_____

_____

_____

_____

_____

_____

_____

CHAPTER SIX
THE EMPTY CROSS

The Empty Cross

The Crucifix and the Cross

As the empty Cross symbolizes so much to our Christian journey, the following is meant to share my deepest personal beliefs and understanding of that symbol.

Jewelry designers, sculptors, and clothing manufacturers have (over the years) shown Jesus Christ, our **RISEN** Savior, nailed on a cross. The information that follows is not meant to criticize or change anyone's religion or beliefs; however, it is meant to share an important *fact* which some may not have thought about.

Christians believe that our Savior, Jesus Christ, was taken off Calvary's Cross, laid in a tomb, and on the third day after his crucifixion, rose again. For Jesus to be displayed on a cross with a crown of thorns is not scripturally correct. **HE IS NOT ON A CROSS ANYMORE!** That is why we celebrate Easter (or Resurrection Day)!

The scripture quote written by Paul from Colossians 3:1 makes it quite clear where Jesus is: "If ye then be risen with Christ, seek those things which are above, *where Christ sitteth on the right hand of God*" (emphasis added).

Keeping It Real: The Straight and Narrow

Questions for Consideration

1. Have you ever thought about the empty cross and Jesus not being there and suffering anymore? Explain your thoughts.

_____

_____

_____

_____

_____

_____

_____

_____

_____

_____

_____

_____

_____

_____

_____

2. Is your belief that Colossians 3:1 is incorrect? Should you have a different belief? Explain.

_____

_____

_____

_____

_____

_____

_____

_____

_____

_____

_____

_____

_____

_____

_____

_____

_____

CONCLUSION

It is imperative that we be "real" in our worship to God and His Precious Son, Jesus Christ. This includes interactions with our brothers and sisters who are not only within the body of Christ, but also those who are without the ark of safety found through salvation. As an old saying goes, "Sometimes, the only sermon a person may see is you!" We never know who may be turned away from or drawn into Christianity by our actions and words.

While each journey is unique, the goal is the same. We are to be witnesses while here on Earth and draw others to Jesus Christ. Plant seeds of love and have compassion as you and I point others to Heaven!

BENEDICTION

Colossians 3:16-17 (KJV)

"Let the word of Christ dwell in you richly in all wisdom; teaching and admonishing one another in psalms and hymns and spiritual songs, singing with grace in your hearts to the LORD.
And whatsoever ye do in word or deed, do all in the name of the Lord Jesus, giving thanks to God and the Father by him."
Amen.

TESTIMONIES and INSIGHTS

Written reviews and comments are provided from some who have shared inspirations and strength received from reading my two previous books *Spiritual Growth: From Milk to Strong Meat* and *Believing Without Seeing: The Power of Faith.*

Rev. Margaret Jackson, Pulpit Staff, Tabernacle Baptist Church
"Marlowe: Thank you for sharing your heart. Your publication, Spiritual Growth: From Milk to Strong meat, is encouraging and inspirational. I applaud you for your willingness to stand up for the Kingdom of God, sharing your poetry and life experiences."

Claretha Mervin, Educator and Youth Mentor
"I enjoyed reading Spiritual Growth from Milk to Strong Meat and I would recommend it to any of my friends. This book was an encouragement to me letting me know every day is not going to be easy, but I can grow as I go through the storms of life."

Cousin Marian Wynder, Missionary President, AME Church Member
"Spiritual Growth: From Milk to Strong Meat was very good reading for all ages. The journey the book took us on was informative, insightful and relatable. I shared the book with a friend who also enjoy it and was inspired."

Keeping It Real: The Straight and Narrow

Beverly Jackson, CMSgt (Ret)
"I loved Spiritual Growth: From Milk to Strong Meat. I know Marlowe Scott personally and she walks the life she wrote about. A lot of her experiences are shared in the book I found relates to my life also. She just poetically put it in a very interesting format to bring humor to her life experience in lieu of sadness. I have read it again and again on down days to bring me back to reality and remind me how blessed I really am. I purchased several copies and gave as gifts to my church family members."

Mary Lanterman, Retired Banker and Prolific Quilter
"Inspirational and encouraging reading for sure. With God guiding my life and friends like you to light the path, serenity can only be ahead!"

Elder Valerie Pernell, St. John Pentecostal Church
"My aunt lent me your book. It's absolutely beautiful. It didn't feel like I was reading a book. It felt like I was having a beautiful conversation with the author, YOU. Life's Railroad to Heaven was a song my mother loved and I love it myself, in fact I need to sing this again...it's been a very long time since I sang this song. Please continue to do whatever the Lord instructs you to do."

Jennifer Mervin, Educator
"Your book was an inspiration to me. Some days I become very weary of my faith and began to doubt what God has planned for my life, but when I look back over my life and see what God has brought you through, it allows for me to resume my faith in him because he blessed me with so much and has brought me a mighty long way."

CMSgt Henry C. Whitman, Jr., Retired USAF
"Growing up in the Methodist Church and having a special needs relative, I was amazed how indistinguishable many of our life experiences were. Reading your first book, Spiritual Growth: From Milk to Strong Meat was like "COMING HOME".

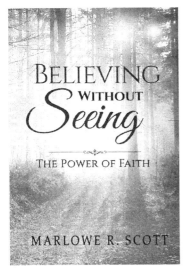

Harry Addison, Jr, Retired Engineer and Church Trustee

"Believing Without Seeing is an inspiring book. Marlowe Scott explains how to use Bible study and our God-given gifts to obtain peace of mind and live a Christian life."

Sally Hatcher, Educator

"Both books were very inspiring to me. There were small spoken words that meant so much to me. The books filled my soul and spirit. They depicted life's layout and the struggles we face day by day. The hard and difficulties on life's journey were captivated. Finally, it was clear on how we as a people should live – love and have faith as ordained by God."

Elder and Cousin Arlene Holden, Bethel Pentecostal Church

"Your books are blessings to those who read them because you wrote them from your life experiences. Through reading your story, others may choose to trust God and approach their everyday lives with positive attitudes."

Amazon Best-Selling Books Written by Marlowe R. Scott

Spiritual Growth: From Milk to Strong Meat
2015 Pearly Gates Publishing, LLC
Angela Edwards, CEO

AMAZON BEST-SELLER
Available for purchase at:
http://bit.ly/MilkToMeat

Believing Without Seeing: The Power of Faith
2015 Pearly Gates Publishing, LLC
Angela Edwards, CEO

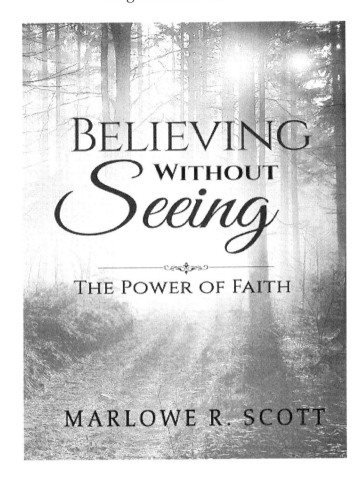

AMAZON BEST-SELLER
Available for purchase at:
http://bit.ly/BelievingWithoutSeeing

Connect with Marlowe!

Marlowe R. Scott
Owner/Creator

Phone: (609) 284-0051
Email: **M.R.BOYCE4491@gmail.com**
Browns Mills, NJ

*"Specializing in Hand-Crafted Creations
Giving Special Comfort and LOVE"*

➢ Memory Pillows

➢ Memory Quilts

➢ Crib Quilts

➢ Throws

➢ And much, much more!

Made in the USA
San Bernardino, CA
24 June 2016